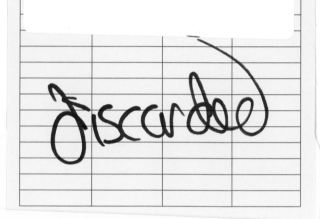

Dolphins, Seals, and Other Sea Mammals

Text by Mary Jo Rhodes and David Hall
Photographs by David Hall

Undersea
Encounters

Children's Press®
A Division of Scholastic Inc.
New York   Toronto   London   Auckland   Sydney
Mexico City   New Delhi   Hong Kong
Danbury, Connecticut

Library of Congress Cataloging-in-Publication Data

Rhodes, Mary Jo, 1957-
   Dolphins, seals, and other sea mammals / Mary Jo Rhodes and David Hall; photographs by David Hall.
      p. cm. (Undersea encounters)
   Includes index.
   ISBN-10: 0-516-24392-6 (lib. bdg.)   0-516-25352-2 (pbk.)
   ISBN-13: 978-0-516-24392-4 (lib. bdg.)   978-0-516-25352-7 (pbk.)
   1. Marine mammals—Juvenile literature. I. Hall, David, 1943 Oct. 2– II. Title.
III. Series.
   QL713.2.R513 2006
   599.5—dc22

                              2005024776

For researchers and others who are working to save these gentle and intelligent animals
and for the next generation who must continue the task.
—D. H.
To my friend Roger Ansanelli, singer extraordinaire, who encouraged me to sing my own song.
This one is for him.
—M. J. R.

All photographs © 2007 by David Hall except: Brandon Cole Marine Photography: 29, 32, 33, 37; Corbis Images/Stuart Westmorland: 4, 5; Minden Pictures: 43 (Tim Fitzharris), 1, 3 top right, 8 (Michio Hoshino), 11 inset, 15 bottom (Frans Lanting), 10, 11, 35 (Flip Nicklin); Nature Picture Library Ltd.: 25 (Doug Perrine), 36 (Doc White); Seapics.com: 34 (Phillip Cola), 24 top (Doug Perrine); Yva Momatiuk & John Eastcott: 15 top, 18, 20, 42.

Dolphins are highly intelligent mammals.
pg. 30

The thick fur on this baby harp seal helps to keep it warm.
pg. 8

Dolphins, Seals, and Other Sea Mammals

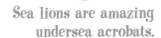

Sea lions are amazing undersea acrobats.
pg. 12

Two bottlenose dolphins leap out of the water. Dolphins may look a lot like fish, but they are mammals.

chapter 1

What Is a Sea Mammal?

A swimming dolphin leaps above the waves and spins in midair. A sea lion flies through the water using its flippers like wings. A manatee grazes in an undersea meadow. Dolphins, sea lions, and manatees are as comfortable in the water as fish. Yet these animals are not fish. They are mammals that live in the sea.

Like other sea mammals, a mother sea lion teaches her pup how to survive in the ocean.

What Is a Mammal?

Dolphins, manatees, and sea lions are more like humans than fish. Like us, they are mammals. Mammals give birth to live young. They do not lay eggs like most fish. Fish may lay thousands of eggs. After they hatch, baby fish are on their own. But sea mammal mothers usually have just one baby at a time. They nurse their babies with milk for weeks or months. They also protect their young and teach them how to survive.

Sea mammals, also called **marine** mammals, are not able to breathe underwater as fish do. Instead, sea mammals hold their breath while they are

Unlike a fish, a manatee must come to the surface every few minutes to breathe.

underwater. They must come to the surface for air.

Mammals are warm-blooded. That means their body temperature is constantly regulated by processes that take place inside their bodies. Unlike fish, a sea mammal's body remains warmer than the ocean water. Most sea mammals have a thick layer of fat, or **blubber**, under their skin. This fat helps to keep them warm.

A thick coat of fur helps this baby harp seal stay warm. Mammals are the only animals with hair or fur.

Some sea mammals, such as sea otters and seals, have thick fur that also helps keep them warm. But other sea mammals, such as manatees, whales, and dolphins, have very little hair.

From the Sea to the Land and Back Again
Scientists believe that life on Earth began in the sea more than three billion years ago. About 350 million years ago, the ancestors of mammals left the sea to live on land. Beginning about 55 million years ago, some mammals returned to the sea.

We don't know for certain why some animals returned to the ocean. Perhaps they were looking for food or were escaping from **predators**. We do know that over many generations, their bodies gradually changed. These mammals became more and more **adapted** to life in the sea.

Today, there are several different kinds of mammals living in the sea. Some, such as sea otters, still look a lot like their land cousins. Others, such as dolphins, have lost their legs and look more like fish.

The ancestors of dolphins were land mammals that returned to the sea more than 50 million years ago.

Life at Sea

Polar bears and sea otters don't look like typical sea mammals. Except for their color, polar bears look like bears that live on land. Sea otters look like the otters that live in freshwater lakes and rivers. Yet both of these animals depend on the sea for their food. Sea otters live entirely at sea, while polar bears spend much of their time floating on large pieces of sea ice.

Polar Bears

Polar bears live in the frozen Arctic, including northern Canada and Greenland. They are the largest of all bears. Males can be more than 8 feet (2.4 meters) tall when standing upright and weigh 1,500 pounds (680 kilograms) or more.

Unlike land bears, polar bears have partially webbed front paws. Like most other sea mammals, polar bears have a layer of blubber under their skin that helps keep them warm.

Polar bears hunt and eat seals. They are able to swim many miles from one section of sea ice to another.

A sea otter mother nurses her baby while floating on her back. Sea otters are the smallest of the sea mammals, about the size of a large dog.

Sea Otters

Sea otters are found along the Pacific Coast of North and South America. They live mainly on the surface of the ocean, resting among giant kelp (tall seaweed) plants. When they are hungry, otters dive to the sea bottom in search of crabs, sea urchins, and other shellfish.

Sea otters have webbed flipperlike hind legs. They seldom leave the water and are clumsy on land. Otters mate, give birth, and nurse their young in the sea. Sea otters do not have blubber, but they do have the thickest fur of any mammal.

Polar bears spend much of their time floating on sea ice while hunting for seals.

11

Sea lions may look clumsy on land, but they are graceful and powerful swimmers.

chapter 2

Seals and Sea Lions

Have you ever seen a trained sea lion balancing a ball on its nose? Waddling around on four flippers, it may seem clumsy. In the water, however, it is one of the most graceful and athletic animals in the sea.

Sea lions, along with true seals and walruses, belong to a group of sea mammals called **pinnipeds**. (*Pinniped* means "wing-footed.") Scientists believe that pinnipeds may be distantly related to bears.

Pinnipeds appear even better adapted to ocean life than sea otters. Both their front and back limbs have become flippers. All pinnipeds, however, leave the water to rest and warm themselves in the sun. Most seals and sea lions also mate, give birth, and nurse their young on land.

Like all mammals, sea lion mothers nurse their babies.

Where Do Pinnipeds Live?

Pinnipeds are found in all oceans of the world. Most live in cool or cold seas, including the icy waters of the Arctic and the Antarctic. A few **species** of seals, called monk seals, live in warm, tropical seas. Most seals and sea lions depend partly on their fur for warmth. Fur seals, a type of sea lion, have especially thick fur.

Pinnipeds range in size from the male southern elephant seal, which may be 15 feet (4.5 m) in length and

Weddell seals live in Antarctica. They are protected from the cold by thick fur and by blubber under their skin.

Male elephant seals are the largest pinnipeds and also the deepest divers.

15

weigh nearly 8,000 pounds (3,629 kg), to the freshwater Baikal seal, which is less than 5 feet (1.5 m) long.

Seal or Sea Lion?

One way to tell seals apart from sea lions is by their ears. Only sea lions and fur seals have ear flaps that you can see.

Another way is to watch how they move. On land, true seals flop on their bellies, using their clawed front flippers to pull themselves along. Sea lions are able to walk on all four limbs. In the water, seals swim by sweeping their rear flippers from side to side. Sea lions swim by using their strong front flippers like wings. They use their rear flippers to steer.

Sea Mammal Fact

Elephant seals can dive more than 5,000 feet (1,524 m) below the surface and hold their breath for more than an hour.

You can tell a seal from a sea lion by looking for its ears. The Galápagos sea lion (top) has visible ear flaps, while the gray seal (bottom) does not.

The tusks of a walrus are teeth that can be up to 3 feet (1 m) long. Walruses live in the Arctic and use their tusks to pull themselves up onto the ice.

A walrus walks like a sea lion but has no visible ears. Weighing up to 3,000 pounds (1,361 kg), walruses are the largest pinnipeds after elephant seals.

Walruses don't have fur and need to spend lots of time warming themselves in the sun.

Two sea lions greet one another on a beach in South Australia. The one on the left has scars on its body from the bite of a great white shark.

Predators and Prey

Like otters, seals and sea lions are predators. They dive to hunt fish, squid, crabs, and other sea animals. Some seals are able to dive hundreds or even thousands of feet in search of a meal. A diving seal can hold its breath for a long time. It is able to store extra oxygen in its blood and muscles.

Seals and sea lions are, in turn, hunted by some of the ocean's most feared predators. They are among the favorite **prey** of killer whales, polar bears, and great white sharks.

Born on Land

Sea lions and some seals spend part of the year on land in a **rookery**. This is usually a protected beach where the animals return to mate and to give birth.

A sea lion mother nurses her baby for six months to one year. She may leave her baby on land while she hunts for food in the ocean. When she returns, she can recognize her pup among hundreds of others by its cry and its smell.

Hundreds of northern fur seals come to this rocky beach every year to mate, give birth, and nurse their young. It is easy to tell males and females apart because the males are much larger.

Having Fun Underwater

Young sea lions love to play. They play
with each other, with other animals, and
with objects they find in the sea. As this
sea star was being photographed, a young
Galápagos sea lion swam over to see what
was going on. The sea lion picked up the
sea star and played with it for several
minutes before putting it back down.

Manatees are slow-moving
sea mammals distantly
related to elephants.

chapter 3

Manatees and Dugongs

Manatees and dugongs are **sirenians**, sea animals distantly related to elephants. They are the only sea mammals that are not predators. Sirenians graze on sea grasses, so they are sometimes called sea cows.

Manatees and dugongs have lost their hind legs completely and never leave the water. Manatees have paddle-shaped tails, while dugongs have forked tails similar to the tail of a dolphin.

A dugong has a forked tail like the tail of a dolphin.

Dugongs average about 9 feet (2.7 m) long and weigh about 600 pounds (272 kg). Manatees are a bit longer and twice as heavy. Both are slow-moving animals. Manatees usually travel alone or in small groups, while dugongs sometimes form large herds.

Unlike a dugong, a manatee has a paddle-shaped tail.

Living in Warm Water

In spite of their large size, sirenians do not have much blubber to keep them warm. In the United States, manatees are found mainly in the seas around Florida. In the winter, they swim up rivers where the water is warmer.

Manatees also live in the West Indies, South America, and West Africa. Dugongs are found throughout the tropical Pacific and Indian oceans, from New Guinea to Africa.

Manatees nurse their babies in the water. The mother's mammary (milk) glands are located in her armpits!

The sperm whale is the largest toothed whale. This young male's teeth have not yet grown in, but he is already as long as a school bus.

chapter 4

Dolphins and Toothed Whales

Diving deeper than any other air-breathing animal, a sperm whale can descend more than 9,000 feet (2,745 m) in search of its prey. Guided by a kind of radar, it hunts deep-sea squid and fish in the dark ocean depths.

Sperm whales are **cetaceans**, members of a group of sea mammals that includes all whales and dolphins. Like sirenians, cetaceans have no rear limbs at all. They have developed tail fins

Dolphins have a dorsal fin, two pectoral fins, and a pair of tail fins called flukes.

called **flukes**. Most cetaceans also have a fin on their backs, known as a dorsal fin, similar to those of fish.

Of all sea mammals, cetaceans are the ones that are most fully adapted to life in the sea. Although they look a lot like fish, cetaceans are distantly related to hoofed mammals such as hippos.

Whales with Teeth

There are two kinds of cetaceans: those with teeth and those without teeth. All cetaceans with teeth are called toothed whales. They include oceangoing and river dolphins, killer whales, **porpoises**, belugas, and sperm whales.

Toothed whales range in size from the 5-foot (1.5-m) vaquita porpoise to the giant—nearly 60-foot (18-m)—sperm whale. Toothed whales are predators that hunt fish, squid, and other prey.

Toothed whales live in all of the world's oceans. Most, such as sperm whales, live in the open sea. Porpoises and many types of dolphins live near land. Belugas, or white whales, are found in cold Arctic waters, while spotted dolphins live in the tropics. Not all toothed whales live in the ocean, however. River dolphins live in freshwater rivers in South America and Asia.

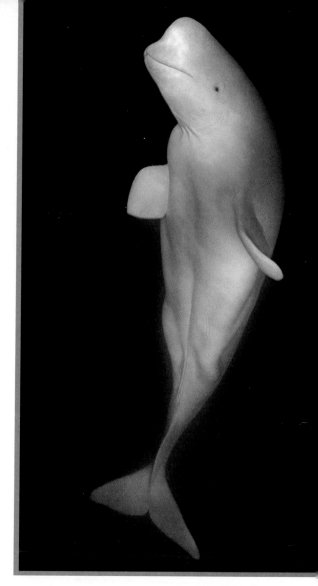

White whales, or belugas, are toothed whales that live in cold Arctic waters.

A mother whitesided dolphin nurses and protects her calf until it is at least one year old.

Smart Dolphins

Toothed whales are among the most intelligent of all mammals. Dolphins have been taught to retrieve lost objects from the ocean floor. In aquariums and marine parks, they quickly learn to perform acrobatic stunts.

The orca, or killer whale, is the largest member of the dolphin family. It is the ocean's top predator, and will attack even the largest sharks and whales.

Social Mammals

Most toothed whales are highly social animals. Many live in small groups called **pods**. Spinner and common dolphins travel in large groups of several hundred animals. The animals may stay together for protection against predators, for finding food, and for breeding.

Dolphins in a pod work together when hunting. They will also help injured or sick members of the pod by pushing them gently to the surface so they can breathe.

Spotted dolphins are social animals that live in small groups called pods.

Seeing with Sound

Toothed whales have a remarkable ability called echolocation. They are able to "see" in dark or murky water using sound waves. A dolphin directs clicking sounds at something in the water, such as a fish or another dolphin. It listens for the echoes as these sounds bounce back. From the echo pattern the dolphin can determine the shape, size, and distance of anything underwater.

The large bump on the front of a beluga whale's head is called the melon. The melon may help some whales to focus the beam of sound used for echolocation.

This humpback whale is breeching, or leaping clear of the water. Humpbacks may breech to demonstrate their fitness to other whales or, perhaps, just for fun.

chapter 5

The Great Whales

Imagine a sea mammal that is as long as three school buses lined up. Its heart is the size of a small car, and its tongue weighs more than an elephant. This cetacean, the blue whale, is the largest animal that has ever lived. An adult may be nearly 100 feet (30.5 m) long and weigh close to 150 tons (136,077 kg)!

The blue whale and its relatives are **baleen** whales. Baleen whales are cetaceans that have no teeth. Instead,

The blue whale is the largest animal that has ever lived. Like other baleen whales, it breathes through a pair of blowholes on the top of its head.

they have a series of fringed plates in their mouths that are used for feeding. Baleen whales breathe through a pair of openings called blowholes on the top of the head. Toothed whales have just one blowhole.

Big and Bigger

There are three kinds of baleen whales: right whales, gray whales, and **rorquals**. Right whales were named by whalers because they are easy to catch, and their bodies float after they have been killed. This made them the "right" whale to hunt. Right whales have a very large head and no dorsal fin.

A curious gray whale approaches a boat.

The California gray whale also lacks a dorsal fin. It has light-colored patches of barnacles and whale lice living on its skin. Gray whales are sometimes curious and may approach a boat closely to have a good look.

Rorquals are long, slender whales that can swim very fast. There are several kinds, ranging from the 26-foot (8-m) dwarf minke whale to the huge blue whale. Other rorquals include the fin, sei, Bryde's, and humpback whales. Rorquals have throats with skin folds that can expand like

The blue whale's throat has skin folds or pleats that allow it to expand like a balloon when the whale is feeding.

a balloon. This allows them to take in a lot of water while they are feeding.

A Big Appetite

Blue whales eat small animals called krill in very large quantities. Krill typically range from 1 to 2 inches (2.5 to 5 centimeters) long and are related to shrimps. A blue whale may eat 3 tons (2,722 kg) or more of krill in a single day. Other baleen whales, such as humpbacks, feed on schools of herring or other small fish.

Baleen whales have enormous mouths with meshlike plates hanging down from their upper jaws. These baleen plates are made from the same material as human fingernails. The plates work like a giant net. When a whale opens its mouth, seawater rushes in and small animals get caught on the baleen.

A humpback swims to the surface with its mouth open, catching many small fish at one time.

Whale Talk

Baleen whales do not use echolocation, but they make sounds. These sounds can carry for many miles underwater and are used for communication. Male humpback whales produce complex combinations of sounds called songs. It is believed that these songs are used to attract a mate.

Whales also communicate with body language. A male humpback will slap the water surface with his powerful tail or pectoral fin. This may serve as a challenge to other males.

A female humpback whale is accompanied by a male who hopes to mate with her.

Breeching, or jumping completely out of the water, may be done just for fun or to remove skin **parasites**. During the breeding season, males may jump as high as possible out of the water as a way of advertising their strength and fitness.

Humpback whales sometimes slap the surface of the water with their tail flukes. This is thought to be a means of communication.

World Travelers

Baleen whales **migrate** long distances. They travel from summer feeding grounds in cold water to warmer seas, where they mate and give birth. For example, many North Atlantic humpbacks travel from Canada to the Caribbean each year. California gray whales migrate as much as 6,000 miles (9,656 kilometers) from Alaska to Mexico. Some migrating whales may be guided by a magnetic sense that works like a compass.

A mother humpback whale with her calf. Humpbacks migrate to warmer waters, where the female whales give birth in the winter.

Humans often feel a bond with dolphins and other sea mammals because they are like us in many ways.

chapter 6

Sea Mammals and People

Sea mammals are our closest relatives in the ocean, but we have not treated them well. We have hunted the great whales for food, oil, and baleen. We have killed seals and sea otters for their fur. Millions of dolphins have been drowned in nets meant to catch tuna.

Some of the few remaining Florida manatees are killed or injured each year by the propellers of powerboats.

This young fur seal is being slowly strangled by a torn piece of fishing net.

Fishing nets and plastic garbage entangle and kill many cetaceans and pinnipeds. Many great whales are injured or killed by collisions with large ships. Pollution of rivers is killing belugas and river dolphins, and threatens all marine life.

Gone Forever

Some sea mammals have become rare and some have already disappeared. There are few remaining Yangtze River dolphins and northern right whales. The Caribbean monk seal and Steller's sea cow (a large manatee) were both hunted to **extinction**.

Are We Doing Enough?

Sea mammals do have many human friends. In 1972, the U.S. government passed the Marine

Sea otters were near extinction one hundred years ago. Now they are protected by law, and the number of otters is increasing.

Mammal Protection Act. It is now against the law to kill or disturb a sea mammal in U.S. coastal waters.

Sea otters and gray whales were hunted almost to extinction by the early 1900s. Now under protection, both have made a strong comeback. If we all work together, it may be possible to save more of our endangered sea mammal relatives.

Glossary

adapted (**uh-DAP-ted**) slowly changed over many generations to allow a better chance for survival and reproduction. *(pg. 9)*

baleen (**bay-LEEN**) fringed plates that hang down inside the mouth of a whale and strain seawater to remove small food animals; whales that feed in this manner are known as baleen whales. *(pg. 33)*

blubber (**BLUH-bur**) the fat in a sea mammal under its skin that helps to keep the animal warm and can also serve as a source of energy. *(pg. 7)*

cetaceans (**si-TAY-shuhnz**) members of a group of sea mammals that includes whales and dolphins. *(pg. 27)*

extinction (**ek-STINGK-shuhn**) the act of becoming extinct or ceasing to exist. *(pg. 42)*

flukes (**FLOOKS**) the tail fins of a cetacean. *(pg. 28)*

marine (**muh-REEN**) living in or having to do with the sea. *(pg. 6)*

migrate (**MYE-grate**) to move from one region to another, usually for feeding, breeding, or because of seasonal weather changes. *(pg. 39)*

parasites (**PA-ruh-sites**) animals or plants that get their food by living on or in another living thing. *(pg. 38)*

pinnipeds (PIN-uh-pedz) a sea mammal group that includes true seals, sea lions, and walruses. *(pg. 13)*

pods (PODZ) groups of dolphins or whales that live together. *(pg. 30)*

porpoises (POR-pus) members of the dolphin family with flattened teeth; most porpoises are smaller than dolphins and have a shorter beak. *(pg. 29)*

predators (PRED-uh-turz) animals that hunt and kill other animals for food. *(pg. 9)*

prey (PRAY) an animal that is hunted and killed for food. *(pg. 19)*

rookery (ROO-kuh-ree) a place where animals gather each year for breeding. *(pg. 20)*

rorquals (ROR-kwilz) generally large, fast-swimming whales with pleated throats and a dorsal fin; blue, fin, sei, and humpback whales are rorquals. *(pg. 34)*

sirenians (si-REE-nee-enz) members of a group of sea mammals that includes manatees and dugongs. *(pg. 23)*

species (SPEE-seez) a particular kind of animal or plant. *(pg. 15)*

Learn More About Dolphins, Seals, and Other Sea Mammals

Books

Becker, John E. *Manatees*. San Diego: KidHaven, 2003.

Bingham, Caroline. *Whales and Dolphins*. New York: DK Publishing, 2003.

Parker, Steve. *Seal: Habitats, Life Cycles, Food Chains, Threats*. Chicago: Raintree, 2003.

Web Sites

American Cetacean Society
(www.acsonline.org)

Friends of the Sea Otter
(www.seaotters.org)

The Marine Mammal Center
(www.tmmc.org)

The National Marine Mammal Laboratory's Education Web Site
(http://nmml.afsc.noaa.gov/education/default.htm)

Save the Manatee Club
(www.savethemanatee.org)

Index

About the Authors

With degrees in zoology and medicine, **David Hall** has worked for the past twenty-five years as both a wildlife photojournalist and a physician. His articles and photographs have appeared in hundreds of calendars, books, and magazines, including *National Geographic, Smithsonian, Natural History,* and *Ranger Rick.* His underwater images have won many major awards, including Nature's Best, BBC Wildlife Photographer of the Year, and Festival Mondial de l'Image Sous-Marine. To see more of David Hall's work, visit www.seaphotos.com.

Mary Jo Rhodes received her master's degree in library service from Columbia University and was a librarian for the Brooklyn Public Library. She later worked for ten years in children's book publishing in New York City. Mary Jo lives with her husband, John Rounds, and teenage sons, Jeremy and Tim, in Hoboken, New Jersey. To learn more about Mary Jo Rhodes and her books, visit www.maryjorhodes.com.

About the Consultant

Doug Perrine has a master's degree in marine biology and has participated in scientific research on whales, sharks, and sea turtles. He has worked as a consultant for films produced by the National Geographic Society and the Discovery Channel. Doug is the author of numerous articles and seven books on marine life, including *Whales, Dolphins & Porpoises.*